Into The Valley And Out Again

By Richard Edler

The story of a father's journey.

Copies of this book may be obtained from:

The Compassionate Friends Resource Center
900 Jorie Boulevard
Oak Brook, Illinois 60522

Phone: (630) 990-0010
Fax: (630) 990-0246

Library of Congress Catalogue Card Number: 96-94457

ISBN 0-9652731-8-0

Cover Photo: Kunio Owaki
Printed in the United States of America
3 5 7 9 10 8 6 4

When you grieve, you have to walk through the valley.

You cannot camp there.

– Dr. Charles L. Heuser
Pilgrimage In Faith

Other books by Richard Edler:

If I Knew Then What I Know Now
G.P. Putnam's Sons. 1995.
ISBN: 0-399-14092-1

Living on Purpose (with William C. Bean)
Safe Harbor Publishers. 1994

With gratitude to The Compassionate Friends,
and other friends who walked beside us.

Richard, Kitty, and Rick Edler

Dedicated to all children gone too soon, including:

Alice Marie Abramson • Ron Acker • Gregg Adams • Larry Joe Adamic • Aaron Seth Anderson • Kya Marisa Anderson • Chelsea M. Anderson • Robert Apodaca • Simon Baioa • Hilary Ann Bartolomeo • Tom Bauman • Justin Bayless • Bethany Beasley • Michelle Lyna Beatovich • Lauren Kaye Bernardo • Deborah Bender-Rowe • Frank Bergin • Fernando E. Bertran • Justin Biggart • Kyle Lee Bishop • Michael Blahnik • Ryan Blahnik • Sean M. Blake • Sammy Bloom • Donnisha Marie Brown • Kurt Boettcher • Todd Boettcher • Brian Lawayne Brooks • Darren Brunkhardt • Lauren Buchanan • Tony Burack • Don J. Burt • Erin Burt • William Caine • Justin Daniel Carney • Dylan Michael Casey • Jose Causley • Richard "Ricky" Chacon • Heidi Chamberlain • Tommy Chandis • David Chavez • Brady Ching • Mark Choate • Robert Christensen • John Cleary • Kelly Swan Cleary • Robert Scott Colston • Neil Loren Cortez • Christina Angelina Cosby • Ethan Patrick Cowden • Ann Beresford Cox • Tracey Crothers • Ralph Cuellar • Jessica Cunningham • Melissa Daily • Blane S. Davidson • Myriah Joy Dennis • Samantha Dennis • Ara Y. Donikian • Joseph Dowling • Scott Dowling • Joe Drew • Debby Durst • Dennis Durst • Christopher Peter Dyck • Gary Edholm • John Edler • Mark Merryweather Edler • Michael J. Edridge • Marc Eisenberg • Melissa Jo Elmore • Richard Paul Engelman • David John Esquivel • Patricia G. Estergaard • Eric D. Fill • Jimmy Finical-Miner • Patrick Fitzsimmons • Vivienne Morecraft Forbush • Mark Joseph Foss • Russ Franich • Dennis Franich • Tara Franich • Kati Franich • Gregory Lynn Gayton • Dennis Lynn Gerringer • Paige Gibson • Steven Giuliano • Stephen E. Goodyear • Alberto Gramirez-Gramirez • Robert Ryan Gruber • Amy Gulak • Geneva Geyer • Damion Haggans • Anthony Hamilton • Nicolas Sherman Hammer • Hrvoje Han • Ivonne Hansen • Robert Belmares Harris • Daniel Hassley • Alicia M. Hayes • Amber M. Hernandez • Robert Joseph Henry • Thomas E. Hill III • Richard Michael Houle • Jeremy Michael Howard • Rachel Hoyt • Maria Hudson-Wells • Richard Huey • Chad Michael Huisinga • Giovanna Iaia • Maki Irimajiri • John E. James • Mark Jensen • Melissa Gale Jetton • Edwin J. Kaslowski • Matthew August Kasper • Scott Ira Kaufman • Tracy Keldebeck • Craig Kelford • Christopher Keller • Jeff Alan Kelly • Kathryn Anne Kelly • Tracy Kildebeck • Heidi Milewski Koolmees • Keith Konopasek • Scott Kovas • Aaron Zev Kushner • Nicolette May La Forrest • Alan Lambie III • Rebecca Lee • Wendy Levine • Barbara Lippen • Stephanie Loder • Stephen Loder • Rick Long • Jeremiah Luddington • Mychal Adair Lynch • Frank Martinez • Kurt Darol Martyn • Toby B. Mattson • Angela Brooks Mayhall •

Michael Patrick McAtee • Jim McGuire • George L. Mc Hay • Richard Meadows • Debra Meighen • Damion Mendoza • Christopher J. Mericle • Shannon Middleton • Michael A. Morgan • Ryan Morris • Allison Najarian • Randy Nance • William Nelson • Israel Nhjera • Jerome Douglas Oliver • William Cole Osborn • Sally O'Toole • Melissa Brown-Pedroza • Robert Pedroza Jr. • Gabriella Pekich • George Arthur Pellegrin • Marv Peterson • Robin Phillips • Justin Phillips • Rachel Phillips • Jennifer Pizer • Anthony R. Ponce • Tom Potter • Leah Ann Priest • Eric Probolsky • David Bruce Ramey • Daniel Paul Rains • Kelly C. Rastello • David Redar • Carole Redman • Linda Redman • Julie Ann Reed • Laura Richardson • Ricky Rivers • Alicia Rivera • Richard E. Rivers IV • Katriona Robertson • Vicky Lynn Rogers • Christine E. Rojas • Jamie Lloyd Roman • Andrei Romero • Michael Ruggera Jr • Marina Ruggiero • Lisa Sandoval • Filiena Desimone Sanchez-Hernandez • F. Marlow Santos • Eric Stephen Schulz • Robert R. Schroeder • Scott D. Silagy • Cheryl Beth Silverman • Gerald Slater • Dave Snepp • Hayley Tyler Smith • Bridget Zerr Smith • Tom Spralja • Clint Spronk • Brian Stains • Susan Stanley • Sarah Stinnett • Jason Subriar • Joshua Strunk • Dirk Sweet • Jeremiah Tate • Amanda Taylor • Kristi Nicole Taylor • Christopher Thompson • Tommy Thor • Danny Thor • Brian Gregory Trotter • Michael Trudeau • Cindy Towle • Jonathan Michael Troutman • Brad Tudor • Michael Vaia • Paul Joseph Vandever • Stacy Kathleen Van Scoyk • Christa M. Vigil • Eric Douglas Vines • Marisa Ann Vuoso • Rashid Walimu • Christopher Walsh • Shawn Weil • David Whittlesey • Rayea Wilcoxen • Victoria Winchester • Jennifer S. Winkelspecht • Patrick Jack Woodward • Marc M. Ybara • Cheryl Wood •

Chapter One — The First Journey

It was a good day to be alive. The afternoon sun was warm but not too hot to sit outside on the little concrete patio by my father's "retirement" room in Asheville, North Carolina. I had come from Los Angeles to spend a few days with Dad, staying with my sister nearby.

He had been going downhill since Mom died two years earlier, but this was different. His decline was accelerating. My sister said he missed our mother so much that he had just given up on living. I think she was right, but I found it hard to comprehend how anybody could not want to live; to hold on dearly to each new day.

I remember looking at the silver maples outside his patio and marveling at how beautiful each day was to me. I was on top of the world enjoying a wonderful family, job and lifestyle – and at 48 could not imagine life being better.

As a child I had been a closet romantic – loving Wordsworth, Byron and Keats more than the White Sox. Every day "my heart with pleasure filled." And this afternoon was especially nice.

"Look Dad," I said, "it's so beautiful outside. Let's go sit on your patio and talk."

My father graciously declined, laying quietly but fully dressed on his self-made bed in his darkened room.

On the chest and shelves surrounding him were the things he treasured most. After Mom died, Dad sold the house in Arkansas, garage-saled everything he considered temporary in life, and packed the trunk of his Chrysler with the things he valued from 87 years of living.

There wasn't much. A black and white photo – now aged brown in the corners – of the 1923 University of Chicago track team, with Coach Alonso Stag standing proud. Today few people even remember that the University of Chicago once had collegiate sports.

There was a second picture with my mother on their wedding day at the Rockefeller Chapel on the Chicago campus. They both came from wealthy Chicago families until the 1929 crash, and then lost everything. The subsequent depression made my father cling to frugality, conservatism, and the security of his banking job at the Federal Reserve.

Then there was a brass-imitation statue of a number one with a golf ball –*the* golf ball – imbedded inside a circle on top. Dad told his hole-in-one story often.

Finally, there was his Bible, which he read cover to cover. That's all I remember in the room, except a tie tack with the Federal Reserve Bank of Chicago on it, which I now have, and a new television we bought him on one of our trips so he could watch his beloved White Sox.

I avoided talking religion or bringing up my mother's memory. I didn't know what to say about God and it wasn't part of the things we ever talked about in our relatively formal "dictated-letters-to-me-when-I-was-in-college" relationship. I didn't talk about Mom because I didn't want to remind him or hurt his feelings or make him cry. Dad cried when Mom died. It was the only time I saw him cry. I didn't want that to happen again.

We had dinner together, in the center inside courtyard of the nursing home circled by the doors to each resident's own room. This had been a selling point when my sister and I shopped for nursing homes in the Asheville area.

There was a more expensive nursing home nearby but Dad – always happy with a nickel Dairy Queen instead of a quarter cone – said he didn't feel "comfortable" with those rich folks. And besides, this home was smaller and each individual apartment had its own little patio area so each resident preserved some sense of independent living.

At dinner I was Dad's guest and he proudly and loudly introduced me as MY SON FROM CALIFORNIA to all the hearing aids. I counted about 18 hearing aids at five tables silently eating their 5:30 pills and salt-free entrees. Each had his or her own special diet, carefully attended to by the staff.

Dad was, as always, the most gracious and gentle person I have ever known. I am truly proud to be his son. Even at the age of eighty-seven he still got up and helped ladies to their seats, holding their chairs.

Dad had not been there long, but had already established himself as a warm and welcome addition to the strange group of elderly brought together in their last years to this place. In fact, the previous December he had played Joseph in the home's Christmas skit.

Few people came to the Sunday afternoon performance. My sister went and said it was "so sad." Mary couldn't hear, and the angel had a walker, and the shepherds were all women because there weren't enough men, and "Dad looked so foolish in his shawl costume."

After dinner, I had little else to talk about. I told Dad again about his grandsons – Rick's graduation from USC and Mark's academic scholarship to UCLA. I looked about the room for something to buy, but he had everything he needed. I said good night.

I returned to my sisters' for a scotch and "adult" talk (which is different than "elderly talk") and then flew home to LA, promising to visit again after the holidays.

On the evening of December 9, 1991, Dad quietly went around to each retirement apartment and said good-bye to his neighbors. He then walked over and thanked the nurses for all that they had done for him. Then he returned to his room, lay down and joined Mom. His heart just stopped. The head nurse told me later: "Mr. Edler just willed it."

This is the way it is supposed to be. "Dad lived a wonderful life and died peacefully." That's what I said to everybody who called.

Of course I was sad, and I cried. But I was not shaken to my core. This was something I was expecting and prepared for. So were the other children, my sister and brother.

Looking back, I think I was selfishly more sensitive to my own rite of passage at that moment, than to my fathers.' I was stepping up to the front of the family mortality line.

After Dad was cremated, his ashes were sent back to Mountain Home, Arkansas to be buried next to Mom. Kitty and I flew back from LA, arranged a brief memorial service, and placed Dad's ashes in the grave. One of my most vivid memories is how heavy his ashes were. Until you have picked up an urn full of human ashes, you have no idea.

Our two boys – Rick 22 and Mark just 18 – offered to go back with us to Arkansas. I said no stoically, full of myself and the moment. I carefully selected the poem I would read, and saw myself reading it beautifully in my mind's camera.

Neither my brother nor sister came – feeling that they had already said their good-byes to Dad while alive – so Kitty and I were the only family.

When we arrived at the funeral home in Mountain Home for the service there was only one floral arrangement and very few guests, people who lovingly remembered Dad and Mom from their retirement years there. The card on the burgundy carnations said simply: "With love, Mark & Rick".

We never told the boys the name of the funeral home. Somehow they figured it out for themselves. I still have the card among my most precious momentos.

On December 18 we left Arkansas to return home to our real life. And that was that.

I particularly appreciated all the notes of condolence from friends and business associates. My company sent a large donation and flowers too. That impressed me.

Chapter Two — The Second Journey

I read somewhere that if you hang a white T-shirt outside the driver's window of your car, police and other drivers will recognize it as an emergency symbol and give you the right of way. It is the equivalent of a flashing red light for civilians.

I was thinking about that as I drove, but I didn't have a T-shirt and Highway 10 westbound from Palm Desert to Los Angeles was almost deserted at five o'clock on a Saturday morning anyway. It was January 11, 1992, a month after my Father died.

Thirty-minutes earlier I had answered the phone. I was alone in our family condo at a country club in the desert. I had driven out Friday night with a briefcase full of work. Kitty was at a Young Presidents' Organization spouses' seminar in Temecula, near San Diego, so I had several days of uninterrupted sun and work ahead of me.

I loved these mini-retreats by myself. I would get up and jog. Work. Jump in the pool. Work. Jump in the pool. Sit in the sun. Work. Grab some fast food. Work. Watch a movie. Go to sleep.

The phone was two rooms away. I don't really know how I heard it ringing. Nobody calls at 4:30 a.m. with good news so I picked up the receiver cautiously and said "Hello?" with a question mark in my voice.

"Mr. Edler, this is Greg. Mark's had an accident." Greg was Mark's best high school friend and a UCLA fraternity pledge brother at Sigma Chi.

I didn't know then, but he had been trying to reach me for several hours – first at home in Palos Verdes and then, remembering we had a place in the desert, finally tried out here. Greg had even called our local police in Palos Verdes and asked them to go out to our house. Of course they found it locked, dark and empty. So they left.

"Okay Greg, calm down. How badly is he hurt? What happened?"

"He fell. He fell from a wall. I don't know how badly he is hurt but it's pretty bad."

"Greg, where are you now?"

"At a pay phone at the emergency room at UCLA."

"Is the doctor there? Let me talk to the doctor."

"I'll try to get him. Hang on."

The phone went quiet. As I waited I started to make notes on a pad in front of the phone. A week later I would return to these same notes, staring up at me where I had left them on the counter.

Mark
hurt.
fell wall.
UCLA Med center.

The wait was longer than it should have been. Later I would learn that the doctor did not want to come to the phone. It was not that he was callous. Rather just the reverse. He was a new emergency room doctor, and had not yet learned to say the words "Your son died a few minutes ago."

His name was Dr. Rodriguez, and I have never met him. The conversation went like this:

"Mr. Edler."

"Yes, doctor, what happened?"

"Mr. Edler, my name is Dr. Rodriguez, and your son has had a serious accident. He fell from a retaining wall and has sustained head injuries."

"Doctor, I am in Palm Springs and I'm leaving now. Tell me, how serious is it?"

"It's very serious."

"Is it a matter of life and death?"

"Yes."

"Doctor," I said, "do you need my medical insurance number? We have complete coverage and . . . ."

"That won't be necessary now, Mr. Edler, just please come quickly."

Funny. When you are actually in the situation, you miss all the clues. Hope overrides the reality of what people are telling you.

Looking back on this conversation weeks later, I could clearly see the message between the carefully chosen words. At the time I read nothing – absolutely nothing – between the lines. I envisioned Mark sitting up in a hospital bed, like the time he broke his shoulder in freshman football and they shot it full of cortisone. "Hey Dad, look how big my shoulder is."

"I'm leaving now, Doctor," I said. "Take good care of him until I get there." Silence.

I called Kitty. She answered right away, not even sleepy. Kitty is always alert.

"Honey, I have bad news. Mark has been hurt in a fall. Greg called. I don't know how badly he is hurt, but we need to get to UCLA Medical Center. I'm leaving now, but you are closer. We'll talk on the car phones. The doctor said it was very serious. He hit his head. He fell off a wall. You call Rick and I'll call the Larsons" (close friends).

"How could he fall off a wall?" Kitty asked.

"I don't know." I said. "But apparently it was a retaining wall and a few feet on one side and about 30 feet on the other and he fell the wrong way."

It didn't make any sense to me, either.

Next, I called the Larsons. We had called them once when our dog, Pearly, had a heart attack. Kitty and I were at a very important meeting in LA when the kids called and said the dog was having seizures. We left the meeting to hurry home because Rick and Mark were home alone, but called the Larsons just in case. The dog died in our boys arms, and the Larsons helped them through it until we could get home.

The Larsons said they would go immediately to the emergency room. They would be surrogate parents for Mark until we got there.

Then I threw open the trunk of my car and at 4:45 began tossing my clothes, toilet kit, paperwork and whatever into the trunk. I was "packing" in 60 seconds. Just then the security patrol passed by and flashed their spotlight on me. I couldn't blame them. There I was – a fanatical looking man in

his underwear shoveling clothes and stuff into a car –
looking just like a burglary. Petty burglary was a big problem
in desert country clubs because so many absentee owners
only showed up on an occasional weekend, just like me.

And so it began. I left the desert condo about 4:50. I drove to
a gas station – a Union 76 – two blocks away. I didn't have
enough gas to make it back to LA and was mad at myself
because I always believed cars should be put away at night
with full gas tanks – a lesson from my father.

I also returned a rented video, tossing it into the doorway slot
in the video shop next to the gas station. I didn't want it to be
overdue. The mind is a funny thing in a crisis.

The lady inside the glass booth took forever to write my gas
credit card down. I wanted to scream, "My son is hurt, give
me back my damn card." But I just waited. Then I left the
station and merged my company Mazda (our firm did the
advertising for Mazda and all senior executives drove
Mazdas provided by the company) onto Interstate 10
westbound and wound it up to ninety.

It was then I thought about the T-shirt in the window. Much
later I wondered if it would be better to put the shirt outside

the driver's side window or maybe center it above the moon roof so it would flap above the car like a real police light. Or maybe red and a blue T-shirts with one on each side like today's newer police cars.

For the next two hours I never saw a cop. I imagined being pulled over, explaining my emergency, and getting a lights-flashing siren escort. But it didn't happen for me.

It did for Rick.

Our oldest son, Rick, was newly living in his own condominium in Manhattan Beach, about 30 minutes from UCLA and on the ocean. Rick had recently graduated from the University of Southern California and, four years older, was his brother's idol. Kitty reached him from the hotel. She started to explain everything she knew but when she said emergency room at UCLA Rick cut in: "Okay, Mom, I got it. I have to leave now. I'll meet you there."

Rick was always a quick study. When he and Mark were little we used to tell them long stories at bedtime. One evening, obviously ready to get on to something else, Rick looked at his mother and said, "Tonight Mom, can we please just cut to the moral?"

Rick was a lover of cars. He had a used black Porsche 944 and he opened it up on the abandoned early morning 405 Freeway northbound. He got to within a mile of UCLA before he was pulled over for running a red light. He told the cop the truth, and got an escort the rest of the way to the emergency room entrance.

For me, it was very quiet, almost too quiet, on the Interstate driving out of the desert towards an early morning LA. From the car phone I called Lee Reitler, our family doctor and Mark's little league baseball coach years earlier. Lee answered what must have been his one thousandth middle-of-the-night-doctor-at-home phone call.

"Lee," I explained, "this is Rich Edler and I have a confusing message from the UCLA Medical Center. Mark is there and he has been hurt in a fall. Can you call and see how bad it is? I couldn't get a clear answer from a Dr. Rodriguez, and I'm on my way driving in from the desert. Kitty is doing the same, driving in from Temecula." I gave Lee my car phone number and waited.

Ten minutes later, nothing. Fifteen. I talked briefly to Kitty, enough to know we were both triangulating on two different freeways towards UCLA. I told Kitty that I needed the phone clear to wait for Dr. Reitler's call, and hung up.

Lee called back about where the desert sands and windmills melt into the Banning pass.

This is what Lee said: "Rich, I can't find out much over the phone. Sally and I are getting dressed and going to the hospital. I can get more information there."

This is what Lee did not say: "Rich, Sally and I have been discussing what to tell you. Doctor Rodriguez said Mark died a few minutes ago. If I tell you this on a car phone I am afraid you will be unable to drive safely. This means I have to lie to you and it has been a difficult decision for me. But I think it is the right one."

I called Kitty in the car. "Lee just called," I said. " He talked with the doctor and is going to the hospital to meet us there. Where are you?" We checked each other's coordinates and talked about how seriously we thought Mark was hurt. We still had difficulty understanding how you could fall off a retaining wall and we couldn't "picture" the accident in our minds. But in all our discussions – even years later when we asked each other directly – we never thought that Mark

might be dead. It simply was not a conceivable part of our life
picture.

We debated whether to call Kitty's parents in Orange County.
We decided it was serious enough that they needed to be
alerted. Kitty called, and a sixth car began heading towards
the UCLA hospital from another direction – Kitty, Me, Rick,
the Larsons, the Reitlers and now Kitty's parents, with Kitty's
cousin, Nita Allen, driving.

I was, in the popular cliché of the period, a "captain of the
universe." I was in my third presidency of an advertising
agency, and proud that I made more money in one month
than my Dad earned in his best year at the Federal Reserve.

 And Kitty was one of the most successful real estate agents in
California. We lived in a million dollar house. We had
wonderful friends, our health, and most of all two handsome
young men for sons. Each in his own way was remarkable.

Of the two brothers, Mark was the wilder one, living closer to
the edge. He was six feet four and older looking than his
years. His favorite quote was "Learn like you'll live forever;
live like you'll die tomorrow."

Mark was a straight A student and entered UCLA on a partial academic scholarship. He wrote beautiful poetry I was later to discover in his safe in his room, and in poetry-gifts he gave his girlfriend, Jill, which she lovingly shared with us.

Mark was also physically gifted, voted athlete of the year in volleyball in his senior year in high school. He was a leader among his peers, forming his own version of a "Dead Poets Society," called Team Happy Face.

Mark's "symbol" in life was a "happy face," and he drew it on everything. He was both macho and sensitive at the same time, often making his friends stop whatever they were doing to watch the Palos Verdes sunsets. And like a sunset, he blazed brightly.

Mark was also a deep thinker, way ahead of his parents on issues like faith. In his writings it was clear he wrestled with the issue of faith and reason – and had come out on the side of faith.

Mark was once assigned to write a school paper on the person he "most would like to spend a day with." Most of the kids choose a President, a rock singer, or a famous person in the news. Mark choose St. Thomas Aquinas. He wanted to spend his day "arguing faith and reason with him." I don't honestly think the teacher knew what to do with Mark's paper.

Mark raced through his 18 years always seeking new experiences and challenges, almost as if he somehow knew he had less time than others; and so needed to maximize each moment. Mark did everything once – and then rushed on. He had no time for what he called "the small stuff," and he focused intensely on friends and never on collecting "things."

Kitty and I recall fondly a discussion Mark had with the mother of one of his good friends his senior year in high school. Mark was getting straight A's without appearing to be trying. One afternoon she turned to Mark and in exasperation said: "Mark, how do you do it . . . how do you always know the answers?" He thought for a moment and responded, "I don't know how I know, Mrs. Scott, I just know."

And he always did seem to know. His college entrance SATs and volleyball record could have gotten him into Stanford but he didn't want to go there. He wanted to go to UCLA. He told us he wanted to be a part of the real world and go to a state school. He recognized that growing up in Palos Verdes

Estates, a community the *Los Angeles Times* called "the richest suburb of them all," was not representative, and he never took it for granted.

As downtown Los Angeles came into view, and the morning sky lightened behind me, I realized I was only about 40 minutes away. I called Kitty again, and learned she was ahead of me and only about 10 minutes from the hospital.

We both knew that Rick had already arrived earlier, and that our friends, the Larsons, had also reached the emergency room. Not once, did either of us verbalize to each other the obvious question: "Why hasn't anybody called us in our cars?"

Kitty called to tell me she was exiting at Wilshire and would be at UCLA in minutes. I was still 30 minutes behind her. She promised to call.

She didn't. When I exited at Wilshire and turned left into Westwood and UCLA, I pulled alongside the security guard at the university gate and shouted "Where is the emergency room?" He directed me back where I had come a few blocks, then a left and a right. I screeched a U-turn.

Kitty had done exactly the same thing at the same gatehouse a half hour before. When the boys were young, they used to tell us that we always repeated each other. They said I would get home from work and ask the same questions Mom had just asked. The guard at UCLA must have put us together in his mind too, and wondered what was going on.

I pulled into the emergency room parking area and saw Kitty's car. Rick's car was also there as well as some cars I didn't recognize. I parked next to Kitty and rushed inside. I didn't know it then, but everyone was waiting for me.

The only face I saw in the crowd was Kitty's. I will never forget her first words: "Honey, this is the hospital chaplain," she said pointing to a short heavy-set man standing next to her in a beige sport coat.

The next few moments are a blur. I remember the realization that a chaplain can only mean that Mark was dead. I remember falling to my knees with a bunch of arms and legs around me. I remember a compassionate nurse's face.

In the corner was a close friend from Young Presidents' Organization, a special business group we belonged to. He was simply standing there, a quiet testimony to our friendship. His wife had been attending the same seminar with Kitty and had called him at five a.m. He didn't hesitate. He just came.

I saw Rick. I saw friends. I saw nurses. And then everybody ushered and pulled me into a room off the lobby where I could cry and wail. It was the room into which, 45 minutes later, we would pull Kitty's parents who would arrive from Orange County unaware.

Kitty, Rick and I hugged. I am sure of it, but I don't actually remember. What I do remember is a very tall doctor talking to me about "doing everything they could," and "seven doctors worked over him," and "we were able to get his heart to start beating again," and "no brain waves,"and "we massaged his heart" and "I'm sorry."

The doctors and nurses at the UCLA emergency room were wonderful. Unlike many bereaved parents, I carry no anger and only respect for what the medical profession tried to do. Mark was rushed there by ambulance within twenty minutes of his fall – one of the top emergency care facilities in the world. A week later I would send the emergency room a thank you letter – "thank you for doing everything possible to try to save my son's life." They needed to be thanked. So did the ambulance paramedics, but I had no record of who they were.

The head of the emergency room wrote back – saying how much it meant to the staff to get my note and how hard they had tried.

Mark's two best friends were already at the Emergency Room – Greg Shapiro and Darin De Renzis. My questions raged. "What happened?" "How could he fall off a retaining wall?" "Was anybody with him?" "Was he drinking?" I was in shock. I was angry. I was trying to comprehend the incomprehensible. I was trying to do what I had been trained to do as a father and as a husband. I was trying to "fix it."

Kitty and I did make three very important and correct decisions.

First that Mark's girlfriend had to be told immediately. We asked Dr. Reitler, who stood by us watching for signs of shock, to call Jill's home. He knew the family and did so.

Second, we asked if we could donate any of Mark's organs? Why did we think of that? Not out of great altruism but because I believe Mark had talked about it with his mother. I still don't know why the hospital never asked us about transplants since Mark was an 18 year old in perfect health.

I learned later that organs must be harvested – what an incredible euphemism – within the first four hours after death. We must have been borderline. Finally, they said they could use his corneas and we signed a bunch of papers without reading anything.

Third, we said we wanted to see Mark. Yes, to see the body. This seemed to come as a surprise to the nurse, but she also seemed to understand. She said that she would have to check, and we repeated our request so there could be no option to decline. I don't know where we learned the importance of seeing the body, but we somehow knew.

The nurse came back and explained that Mark had been in surgery for a long time, and that this was a university hospital and they had no facilities to prepare the body for viewing and on and on. We repeated our request even more firmly and she agreed.

Mark's grandparents arrived and the process repeated. By now there were fifteen people in the room.

A group of only six formed to see Mark's body: one brother, two parents, two grandparents, and a close relative; all led in tour guide fashion by the senior nurse. We walked into the basement and through drab meandering hallways with pipes overhead for what seemed like forever. It probably was 15 minutes.

We came to a hallway on the left and the nurse guide stopped to warn us again. "We did the best we could do," she said, "but this is a state institution and we have no facilities to view a body."

Kitty, Rick and I rounded the corner. Mark lay there on his back on a gurney in the middle of the hall. The gurney was pulled out from a room I am sure was the morgue. He was in a black rubber body bag unzipped down to his stomach.

Mark's face was calm, but there was a giant white plastic tube sticking up from his mouth like a periscope. It appeared to be shoved into his throat, and was a breathing device, I assume. But to this day I regret not taking it out of his throat, and still wonder why the nurses had not done so.

His body was marked with all kinds of needle holes and his chest was roughly sewn up in several surgical zipper- strips.

Clearly, it was a body on which much attention had been focused a few hours earlier.

It was the saddest moment of my life.

Rick crumpled first. It was the reality of seeing the body – our son and brother – the face we loved, the beautiful black hair, the bushy eyebrows. It was the sudden shock upon shock that this was really true, this was really our Mark, and not a dream. We still did not grasp the magnitude of this moment's impact on our lives. Each of our bodies were furiously pumping out their natural shock chemicals to keep us drugged.

That mental picture – standing in an olive green hallway with pipes overhead and my son in a body bag with a tube in his mouth – is one my mind-camera snapped forever.

Kitty, Rick and I all felt a similar moment of release – as if Mark had been waiting for us to arrive to say good-bye. We felt him floating in the hallway with us. We felt him saying "Now that you are here, I can leave. I have done what I needed to do."

We didn't talk about it then, or even sense it consciously. Yet months later, when we shared our feelings, we each described exactly the same sensation.

We walked out of the emergency room into Saturday morning. Kitty and I insisted on driving together, and our friends took one of our cars. Rick left first, going home to his condo in Manhattan Beach and then promising to come to our house.

Later we would learn from The Compassionate Friends, a wonderful support group for bereaved parents and siblings, that siblings who lose a brother or sister are often called the "forgotten mourners." Everyone rushes to the side of the parents who lose a child, and they tell the surviving siblings to "be strong for your Mom and Dad."

Rick, suddenly losing the brother he loved and thrust into the sudden role of "only child," drove home alone. Who was there for him?

We left the hospital parking lot and, in a neighborhood less than a mile from where I worked and in an area I drove daily for 10 years, I got completely lost. I wandered Westwood, unable to find Wilshire Boulevard which was just three blocks away.

On hindsight, I was deep in shock and should never have been behind the wheel. They should put a warning label on grief that includes the caution: "Do not operate heavy machinery."

When we got close to home we stopped at a little store next to Kitty's real estate office for two diet cokes. I have no idea why to this day. Then Kitty walked next door to her office, calmly checked her messages, and informed the receptionist that her son had just died.

She could have been updating a house listing with the same tone of voice. By now she was in full shock.

We drove the rest of the way home, stopping only once at Mark's girlfriend's house to hug her. It was one of our few moments of clarity that morning.

We called a few family members and friends and that was all. Communications took on a life all their own. Friends called friends. Family called family. The word jumped from college campus to college campus through Team Happy Face.

My boss called from San Francisco within an hour. I was completely taken back by the call, so surprised he knew already on a Saturday.

I remember walking to the back of the house, where our bedroom and private deck was, and sitting outside where no one could see me. I curled up and just shook and cried uncontrollably.

Chapter Three — The Second Day

I worried about Kitty and she about me and we worried together about Rick.

In the first rush of emotions you do not grieve – instead you experience. The reality of the loss has not yet hit. You focus on getting out your child's best picture. "Which frame do you like dear, the gold and silver or the wood? The wood is warmer, don't you think?"

It was almost like a party and we were the hosts. The house was full of people and tears and laughter all at the same time. Laughter seems out of place, but sometimes it is the only thing that gets you through. It's the other side of the grief coin.

There was a practical joke in our family in which people would quietly clip a wooden clothespin on the back shirt or blouse of an unaware victim, who would then walk around looking very silly until he discovered the clothespin. Later in the week as my family gathered, some relatives began this joke again. One even put a clothespin in Mark's suit jacket pocket at the wake, to be buried with him.

I resented the whole clothespin thing, feeling it was in terribly poor taste. Others said it brought some relief to a week where some was badly needed. I still remember it today with discomfort.

Faces of people you never called appear. A best friend and his wife, without asking, flew down from San Francisco, took a nearby motel room, and settled in to "just be there for us" for the entire next week. Another friend, upon hearing the news in his advertising agency corner office in New York, simply walked outside, caught a cab straight to Kennedy Airport, and flew to LA. I will never forget these acts of grace.

In the early days of grief you find you are "performing" better than you really are. You smile and say thank you for coming. You organize things with your office. You say the right things on the phone. But the real you behind the mask is drugged, waiting to wake, come out alone, and grieve for years ahead when all the people and the festivities will be gone.

Losing a child is totally out of order. Children are supposed
to bury their parents, not the other way around. There is a
saying that goes "When you lose your parents you lose your
past; when you lose your spouse you lose your present; but
when you lose a child you lose your future.

I think this is part of what makes the loss of a child so
complicated, and so difficult for someone on the "outside" to
understand. The bereaved parent really grieves three ways.

First, parents grieve for the obvious loss of the child, although
it takes a full six months to come to the realization that he or
she really is gone and not coming back from college; not going
to "just walk through that door."

Second, parents grieve deeply for the child's loss – for the
loss of the life that child would have had and now will never
have – the joys of college, of marriage, of sex, raising children
of their own, and of greeting each new day. This second grief
stays a lifetime as each experience in the future, no matter
how joyful, also carries the shadow sadness of "My child is
missing this."

Third, I think parents grieve privately and silently for the life
they themselves would have had, if that child had lived. I

was not now going to be "Mark's Dad," present tense. It was a title I was very proud of.

I pictured him graduating from UCLA with his mother and I in the audience, entering law school or international business, a great success, marrying well, his brother's best friend, and an integral part of my life as Kitty and I grew older.

Now, Mark's children, our grandchildren, will never be born. His legacy ends on our family tree with a line that just stops without branches. Now all that he would have become and we would have shared as his Mom and Dad is gone. Bereaved parents don't talk about this third level of grief, but it is there.

Day two is also the first day of planning. Questions come up you never expected to think about.

Where is the body and where do you want it to go?

Do you want the body cremated or not?

Where and when will the service be held?

Where will Mark be buried?

What kind of service do you want? What religion? What church?

Who will perform the service?

Who will speak?

What will I say?

On Sunday, January 12, I found myself looking through the yellow pages of the Palos Verdes phone book to find a church and pastor to bury my son. It was probably the single moment in my life where my income was the highest it was ever going to be, and my understanding of what really counts in life was the lowest. It was a watershed moment.

In day two the platitudes began to circle over the house. In the weeks ahead they would hurt in a way the well-meaning never fully understand.

Here are some of the most frequent. People really did say each of these things to us or to other newly bereaved parents we came to know:

"You are so lucky he didn't suffer." Or the reverse, so often said in the case of an extended illness: "You are so lucky you had a chance to say good-bye." Neither is lucky.

"He died the way he would have wanted to." Nobody wants to.

"I know how you feel. I recently lost my grandmother." Sorry, but your loss is part of the natural order of things, while mine is not. We are supposed to go before our children. They are supposed to bury us.

"If there is anything I can do, please don't hesitate to call." You will never be called. We don't have the strength. Instead just look around and find something to do. Don't send a sympathy card; send yourself. Parents won't remember what was said, but they will never forget your face and that you came. Being there is what counts.

"At least you have another child." Or for younger couples "At least you can still have more children." One child can never replace the other.

"It's God's will." or "God must have needed him in heaven." So do we. We need him here. God did not "will" this. He may have allowed it to happen, but he didn't will it.

"You are so strong. God only sends these things to people who can handle them." God, please make me weaker and give me my child back.

"He's in a better place." Maybe, but I want him here. What could be better than being with his Mom, Dad and brother? Heaven can wait.

And even, "What did you do to deserve this?"

Instead of trying to find something good or positive to say, just simply say "I'm sorry."

There is no silver lining in the death of a child. Don't try to find one.

Mark died Saturday morning, January 11. We could not have the memorial service until Thursday, January 16 because it took several days for the Los Angeles County Coroner's Office to release the body. Apparently all bodies in accidents require autopsies and a police report before the body can be released.

Week one is a blur of people, flowers and tears. The delivery boy from the local florist, well on his way to what was to become 78 plants or flowers, asked "Hey, who's getting married here?"

The casserole friends came and came. The honey-baked hams arrived as did our families. Our best friends circled their wagons around our house and handled the hundreds of details from simply answering and screening phone calls to coordinating our wishes with wonderful gentleness. We will forever be in their debt.

Kitty and I picked two pictures of Mark for the memorial card. On the outside was his high school graduation picture –

traditional head and shoulders photo with Mark in a dark suit, white shirt, red tie and looking handsome and focused on his future.

Inside we chose to reproduce a full-length snapshot taken at the same time as the graduation picture. Below the waist Mark's coat and tie ended in pink surfer shorts and bare feet. True to his personality, Mark wore the obligatory uniform for his "head shot," but remained a cool dude the rest of the way down.

The combination of both pictures captured Mark in a special way that made people smile when they opened the memorial card at the church. It was our way of saying "this was one special kid."

We made all the important decisions as a threesome – Kitty, Rick and I. One was selecting a grave site and a casket. The casket was easy because we picked what we all liked regardless of cost. It was cherry wood. Who cares? We also bought the cement enclosure that insures no moisture gets through. What a business.

To pick a grave site you actually get into a little car with a representative from the cemetery – excuse me, memorial park

– and drive around to look at little lots. You talk about things like view of the ocean and shade trees nearby. It was like Kitty showing tiny real estate lots in her business.

We finally selected one area and bought four lots in a row. Like most Californians, we came from somewhere else, and this was the first time we had to make the decision about where "home" really was.

We elected to have the burial Thursday morning and the memorial service Thursday afternoon. This is a little backwards versus tradition, but we wanted a private burial for family and close friends, and a more public memorial tribute to our son after that.

Lots of people told us that it would be important for Mark to have a wake and an open casket so his friends could say good-bye as they gathered from various colleges around the country. We agreed. The wake was set for Wednesday night.

This was also the week to decide what we were going to say at the service. We realized that a lot of people would come to the service because of friendship or business relationships with us, but really would not know much about Mark at all. So we would tell them.

This first week you operate in shock. Yet we managed to operate well on the adrenaline and almost singularly focus on the memorial service. Kitty and I both felt that this was something we wanted to make meaningful; and something we could never do over again if we botched it.

The theme for the whole service was set by Rick when he said to us: "Now that we are a family of three instead of four, we each have to live the rest of our life one-third better."

I don't know where Rick got the strength to reach inside himself and come up with that wisdom, but it marked a turning point for us and became a standard we now live by.

The church was a great help and we were blessed to have Dr. Karl Johnson, Senior Minister at The Neighborhood Church in Palos Verdes, take us under his wing with no regard for the fact that we were not church members and had literally cold-called him. We met under the worst of circumstances, but were to become the best of friends.

There were several things which were automatic for us in planning the service. The first was that the daisy would be Mark's flower. It already was. Years earlier our family had adopted the flower and a quote by Nadine Stair, a 94 year old lady from Louisville, Kentucky. Mrs. Stair had been asked by the local newspaper, "If you had your life to live over, what would you have done differently?"

Her answer became more than a framed passage in our kitchen. It became a way of life for all of us, and particularly for Mark. Mark even used this quote in his entrance essay for UCLA:

> "If I had my life to live over, I would dare to make more mistakes next time. I would relax. I would limber up. I would be sillier than I've been this time. I would take fewer things seriously, and I would take more chances. I'd take more trips; I'd climb more mountains and I'd swim more rivers. I would eat more ice cream, and less beans. I would perhaps have more actual troubles, but I'd have fewer imaginary ones."

> "You see, I am one of those people who lived sensibly and sanely, hour after hour, day after day. Oh, I've had my moments, but if I had it to do over again, I'd have

more of them. In fact, I'd try to have nothing else – just moments – one after another instead of living so many years ahead."

"I've been one of those persons who never goes anywhere without a thermometer, a hot water bottle, a raincoat and a parachute. If I had my life to live over, I would start barefoot earlier in the spring, and I would stay that way later in the fall. I would go to more dances. I would ride more merry-go-rounds. I would pick more daisies."

We picked three songs for the service: *Think of Me* from *Phantom of the Opera* , a musical our whole family loved and went to see together; *Come Sail Away*, a relatively unknown and hauntingly appropriate song by the rock group Styx that Rick selected as one of Mark's favorites; and *Amazing Grace.*

Amazing Grace has always been a song I loved, but not something I talked much about. For Christmas just several weeks before his death and immediately after my Dad's death, Mark gave me a CD of Amazing Grace played by bagpipes.

I was a little surprised at the present, but accepted it with the thank yous appropriate to the assembly line gift opening that was our Christmas ritual. But inside, I was touched deeply by his thoughtful-ness. Later we would remark to ourselves: "It was almost as if he knew."

As we were planning the service, Rick asked that Amazing Grace be one of the songs. He told us about a conversation with his brother a month earlier when Kitty and I were back in Arkansas burying my Dad's ashes.

Mark told Rick that, when he died, he wanted Amazing Grace played as his casket was lowered into the ground. He reasoned, he said, that burials are always done in silence and that seemed wrong. He wanted to hear *Amazing Grace* played good and loud by bagpipes to break the silence. Do most 18 year olds have these thoughts?

A few days after Mark's death, we opened his little blue safe in his room. I felt like an intruder. I never pried into Mark's things, but now there was no one else to open it.

Inside were crumpled pages of high school note paper, with a poem on each page. Later I would also learn of a book of poetry he gave his girlfriend Jill, and which she shared with us. In the book Mark wrote to Jill: "You already have my heart, with these poems I give you my soul."

The poems were beautiful, and a little dark. Reading them without any background, one might conclude the writer was contemplating his own death. We do not think that, but the shadow suggestion is strong enough in Mark's poems that we hesitated to have them published as a group.

The poems represent a special side of our son we never really knew. I have written poetry since I was nine, and yet I did not know Mark did. I feel bad about this, as if I missed a special bond with my son that I cannot recapture. But when you are a teenager, a Dad sometimes must choose between being either friend or father, and cannot be both.

I chose to be a father. And in doing so, I missed being a confidant. I would make the same choice if I had it to do over.

And so I discovered the poems for the first time in that little blue safe with the red dial – spreading them out before me in his room on his bed with tears running down my cheeks as I read each one.

For the Thursday morning burial we hired a lone bagpiper
who, in full kilts and regalia, played Amazing Grace from the
crest of the hill above the gravesite.

Karl Johnson conducted the service and then asked if anyone
wished to say anything. No one spoke. It was an
uncomfortable silence. So I stepped forward, faced the
group, and recited a poem my mother taught me. I had used
it a month earlier in Arkansas.

It is called "Somewhere" and the author is unknown. My
mother picked it out of the *Chicago Tribune* "Line o' Type"
column years ago and passed it down in her handwriting, and
my memory.

> Somewhere in the troubled night,
> When you fight the lonely fight,
> Will you but remember then,
> I am at your side again.
> As I was in other days,
> When we traveled better ways.
> True, I cannot touch your hand,
> But I know you understand.
> Love is not a thing of place,
> Only standing face to face.

Love is, too, a thing of heart.
And though we're dwelling far apart,
There is never far from here.
Here is never far from there,
To the ones who really care.
So, if you loved me, do not grieve,
Those who love, also believe.
If you need me, do but call.
I am with you, after all.

Then everyone put a daisy on the casket. The bagpiper played *Amazing Grace* good and loud. And Mark was buried just as he had asked of his brother several weeks earlier.

That afternoon the memorial service began with 600 people in and standing outside a church that could seat 350 with all the folding chairs set up.

Mark's two best friends – Greg and Darin – each spoke. The Sigma Chi fraternity – 120 young men in crisp blazers – filed down the center aisle and each placed a single white rose on the altar, the Sigma Chi flower. I spoke, Rick spoke, and Kitty closed. We did what we set out to do. We did this day the way Mark would have wanted us to.

After the service I gave the Minister and the soloist each a "tip."

I was still trying to "fix things," applying my old rules about how to do things to a new world where they no longer applied, in a valley where there was no path.

Chapter Five — The Second Week

In week two there are the appropriate questions and the real ones.

The appropriate questions a parent asks are things like "What flowers should we have in the church?" and "Where should we put the collage of his pictures his friends made?"

The real questions are these:

"Did he suffer?"

"What did he think just before he died?"

"Was someone with him?"

"Why wasn't I there?" or if you were, "Why didn't I save him?"

"Where is my child?"

"Why did God let this happen?"

"Can he hear me?"

"Should I go be with him?"

"Will this hurt ever ease? Will this fog ever lift?"

"Will I ever feel happy again?"

"Will I see my child again?"

"What will he look like in heaven and how will we know each other if I get old and he doesn't?"

"How will I ever get to sleep?"

"How will I ever get out of bed?"

"Does anybody really know how I feel?"

"Am I going crazy?"

"Do I care?"

In week two you see your child walking across the street. You see a Nissan Pathfinder truck like his and you follow it for blocks. The phone rings and you think it might be him. You see his friends and he is with them.

You hit the bed, throw the pillows, beat the wall, and scream out loud. You sit motionless, staring blankly at his hairbrush. You bury your face in his clothes to capture the smell.

You replay your last conversation together. If it is a sudden unexpected death, the conversation is never the one you wish you had had. In our case it was seven short words.

"I came back to get my glasses."

These were the last words we heard from Mark. On the Wednesday before the Saturday morning he died he had stopped by the house. After leaving he remembered his reading glasses and drove back to pick them up. I remember walking out with him and waving good-bye from the driveway.

Mark's words are also preserved on tape. The tape is from his answering machine at school. It isn't much. It simply asks the caller to leave a message at the beep. But it is his voice.

And so that little tape cassette sits in our safe deposit box along with our less valuable possessions like stocks and jewelry. Our deposit box must contain the only answering machine tape in the bank.

Perhaps the single most common hope by parents in the first few weeks after the death of a child is for some sort of sign that their child is okay. Parents see their primary job as taking care of their children, and when a child dies they feel they have failed. They worry that he is alone, frightened, and in need of them.

Years later I would find myself spending delicate hours with a grieving father reflectively listening – which is all you can really do – while watching for the signs of suicide. The father felt he needed to "go and be with his son now" so he could help him.

Time and again in the weeks immediately following Mark's death Kitty begged for a sign. "Mark," she would cry while she was driving, "please, please let me know you are okay, honey."

He did. It came in a special way with two dreams from different people on the same day. Kitty looks back on these as messages from Mark which helped her when she needed it most.

The first message was from a real estate business associate of Kitty's who came to her office. This was not a close personal friend, just a professional acquaintance who knew nothing of our family, and had only met Mark once.

She apologized for coming, but said she had a dream about Mark, and felt compelled to come over and tell Kitty about it. She said she had seen Mark, and he was standing there with a short old lady with white curly hair and a big smile and they were holding hands and saying everything was okay.

The lady went on to explain that she did not feel she had the right to come and tell Kitty all of this but she couldn't help herself. She also said she had no idea who the little white-haired woman was.

That lady was my mother. She died several years earlier. I am sure she met Mark at the gate or the tunnel or the end of the light or whatever. Her beautiful white curly hair was always a trademark, as was her wonderful smile. They are the two things I would have used to describe my mother to a stranger.

I know that my mother would be the one to meet Mark. They had a special bond, and he was the grandson carrying on the Merryweather name, which was my mother's maiden name. She was so proud of it, and had traced it back through English aristocracy and eventually to Alfred Lord Tenneyson. My mother had six grandsons, but only Mark was carrying the name into the next generation.

I don't know if there is a tunnel and a bright light or not. But there is something. Dr. Kubler-Ross tells the story of a nine-year old child who came back from near death and told her parents she was met by someone who said he was her brother, but she was puzzled since she did not have a brother.

Her parents then explained that she did, in fact, have a brother who died several years before she was born. They had never told her about it as she was growing up. There are thousands of stories like this. We had one when we needed it most.

The second dream was from Mark's girlfriend's older sister Susan. It occurred about the same time. According to Susan's dream, Mark came back and was having a conversation with her. Susan asked, "Hey Mark, have you seen Jesus yet?"

"Seen him?" Mark exclaimed loudly, "You couldn't miss him! And guess what," Mark added, "He even knew my name." I can still see Jesus going out of his way to walk over and say hello to Mark.

Mark didn't impress easily. This would have done it.

Were these dreams real? Were they after death communication? Were they messages from God? Or were they wishful thinking and selective perception by people in shock?

For us they were the first steps towards a deep faith, and absolute confidence in a life after this one.

Chapter Six — Month Two

Kitty promised me she would not commit suicide but, on the other hand, she was not going to make it difficult for a car accident or cancer to claim her.

She refused to wear her seat belt. She would drive along the bluff near our home and think that, with a simple turn of the wheel and a few minutes, she would be with Mark again.

This may be the point in complete depression where if the doctor says you have only a few months to live, you say: "Fine, doctor, but can you hurry it up?"

Two months is when most grief is supposed to start to heal. It is not that way when a child dies. The second month is harder than the first in many ways. And the second six months can be more difficult than the first six.

Month two is also when reality starts to sink in. This is when your good friends understandably go on with their lives, and begin to urge you to "be over it."

I actually had a very close friend and business associate take me out to lunch and tell me "Rich, it really is time now to get over it." He meant well, of course. And because these people are true friends and do not want to see you hurting, they also want to see you heal quickly.

It doesn't happen, at least not yet. At least not for another two years.

By month two the world goes on for everyone else. But bereaved parents are stuck in time. His room is the same. His clothes still hang in the closet. Mail still comes unknowingly addressed to him.

My days were conveniently marked by crying bookends – I would cry in the anonymity of the 405 freeway morning commute to work, listening to Mark's tape of *Amazing Grace,* and then repeat it again on the way home that evening.

During the day I would try to perform the expected "master-of-the-universe" functions of going to work and doing my job. But I was doing a disservice to myself and to my employer. I was only a shell of a person going to client meetings on autopilot.

I was head of an advertising agency of 120 people. They looked to me for leadership and I was running on empty. A year later employees would tell me I was forgetting things. Of course they were right, and of course I don't remember.

I went back to the office one week after Mark died. Work, after all, was what I did, all I knew, and who I was. I sent a staff memo to the office thanking everyone for their condolences. I said I was back now, and our job together was to build our client's businesses. I even said that, since people in the office had asked what they could do to help, that the answer was to get back to work and help grow the agency. I even sent a copy to my boss in San Francisco to show I was back in the saddle.

I was clueless. It was the stupidest memo I ever wrote. Two years later I would read it again and simply shake my head and marvel at how little I knew about what was washing over me.

In addition to the morning and evening commute, my other "safe place" for tears was jogging in the early morning. I have always loved jogging. It is a special time to be alone with myself and my thoughts – almost as good as the freeway, and I could take a shower afterwards so the tears wouldn't show.

One morning while jogging I was thinking about God and where Mark really was. It suddenly occurred to me that God was a bereaved parent, too. I always knew that from Bible stories of course, but until now they had been just that, stories. Now I was able to put it together. I felt all the pain of the Bible passage "God so loved the world that he gave his only son." Suddenly that cliché had substance. How much love God must have had, I thought to myself, to have given up his son voluntarily. And he would not have done so, I reasoned, unless he really had prepared a better place.

It was a surprisingly warm and comforting thought.

Chapter Seven — Month Four

At four months Kitty was able to handle the big things. We could go to church. We could go to the grave. We could go to UCLA.

We just couldn't go down the cereal aisle at Vons.

Mark loved Cherrios. One day in the supermarket Kitty was standing in front of the cereals and a stock boy walked up and asked if he could help. Kitty burst into tears. I'm sure the stock boy felt totally confused: "Hey lady, it's only cereal."

Towards the end of month four the county finally released the autopsy report. It arrived in a brown plain envelope with Department of Coroner, County of Los Angeles stamped on the outside. I sat for a long time and looked at the envelope. Then, after Kitty had gone to bed, I opened it.

Autopsy reports are brutally blunt and direct. They discuss without emotion a "well-developed, well-nourished white male, weighing 201 pounds, body length 76 inches with blunt force head trauma and multiple injuries of brain." The report is accompanied by a preset drawing of a body – sort of like the white police chalk associated with murder mysteries – with all wounds and scars sketched in.

To the coroner there is "an old horizontal scar over the left anterior chin area." To the father reading this, there is a small loving and laughing boy who years ago fell over the handlebars of his bike, landed on his chin in the street, and was rushed to the doctor with his brave mother holding his chin closed while I drove. When the doctor took over and reassured us there would only be a few stitches and Mark would be fine, Kitty fainted.

Much of the wording in the autopsy I could not understand – medical talk. But I did understand that Mark's head injury was so massive that he must have been unaware.

To confirm my interpretation I asked Dr. Reitler to read the report and tell us simply what happened. He called several days later and said, "Mark was immediately knocked unconscious." Lee added "I doubt he even knew he was falling," the prognosis his mother and I so wanted to hear.

I know Lee told us the truth, just as I know it still bothers him to have had to lie to me that morning of my drive in from the desert.

Parents need to know what really happened, as best they can. They need to talk to people who were there, and see the body. They need to visit the site of the accident and understand what their child went through. For the first time I truly understand the anguish of families with a child "missing." Parents need to reach closure and the lack of a physical body or unclear events leave a wound that never heals.

We tried and tried to figure out what really happened at "the wall." How could our son fall a relatively short distance – 26 feet – and die when people fall much greater distances and break an arm or leg? Especially since he was in such perfect physical condition. And why was there no noise? Why didn't he cry out when he slipped? Another fraternity brother walking about 20 steps behind Mark, heard nothing.

For months Kitty and I worried that Mark was afraid or alone, when we should have been there. We constantly relived the twenty minutes between his fall and his arrival at the UCLA emergency room. Who was with him? Was he ever conscious? Did he suffer?

I thought of trying to find the ambulance paramedics to ask them, but I never did.

Month six is when you begin to return to the land of the living. You cautiously accept invitations to a party, decide to go to a business function, and circulate again within your community. And then it comes without warning, and nobody has prepared you for it.

How many children do you have?

This is perhaps the world's most innocent and simple question, part of idle cocktail party talk. And yet it is a knife turner for bereaved parents.

The question raises a real dilemma. First, you know people will ask you that question for the rest of your life at all kinds of innocent meetings, parties and polite dinner table chat. So you have to decide how to handle it.

Second, for example in our case, if we answer "one." we handle the moment but are left with an empty feeling that we have denied our dead child. On the other hand, if we tell the truth – "two children" – we open up the inevitable follow up questions such as "Oh, how nice, and where are they now?"

This seems like such a simple issue. But years later Kitty and I still wrestle with it. For us we finally solved it simply by saying "we had two sons" or we simply answer "two," and try to change the subject. Most people miss the "had" and don't follow up anyway. If people pursue it, we tell them.

When we do acknowledge that one of our children has died, almost nobody asks any more questions beyond a simple "Oh, I'm so sorry."

Actually, parents are crying out to tell their story, to respond to a question such as "What happened?" or "What was your child's name?" or "How long ago?" The bereaved parent really does want to talk about that child, not pretend in a hushed voice that the child doesn't exist and move quickly on to the weather.

Yet our society is taught to give the parents space, and that it would be impolite to probe. It isn't impolite. Please go ahead. Ask about it. Find out the dead child's name and boom it right out loud and clear in the conversation. Parents want desperately to hear their child's name spoken again, and to tell their story.

I still recall the first time I was asked "How many children do you have?" I was on a plane between LA and San Francisco, traveling on business. The businessman sitting next to me asked innocently enough. I froze for a moment, and then answered: "One." He smiled and said something innocuous about his family and went back to his reading.

I sat there with my temperature rising. I had denied Mark. But this man was a passing acquaintance and the story was irrelevant to him. Over Bakersfield I couldn't take it any longer. I turned to him and explained that I had not told him the full story and launched into it non-stop for the next 45 minutes.

When we landed at San Francisco, the poor man grabbed his coat and practically ran off the plane. Just his luck to sit next to me.

Often bereaved parents try to tactfully grant permission to friends who tiptoe around the subject. We throw out permission lines like "What a beautiful sunset. Mark would have liked that." After an awkward pause, the other people relax and usually pick up on it. Once you have said your child's name, you give permission for others to do so too. Bereaved parents have to help the rest of the world know how to react. Nobody means ill, they just don't know. Before our children died, we didn't know either.

Month six is also the month I call "How's Kitty doing?" This is the time people quietly look at me, slip their arm around my shoulder with a knowing hug, and whisper "How's Kitty doing?"

The inference, of course, is that the man has gotten over it, swallowed his grief, stiffened his lip, and moved on to be the strong one in the family. The concern is with the mother's recovery. Nobody asks how I am doing.

And I learned to play my role well. I reassure the person knowingly that Kitty is doing better, and refit my mask. I wait for the commute home. Nobody notices or cares if the guy next to you on the freeway has tears rolling down his cheeks. LA freeways are the safest place in the world for men to cry.

Month six is when I got angry. I was angry at Mark for drinking the night he fell, and at myself for not being a tougher father who not only lectured his sons against drinking, but should have been less tolerant when I knew he was. Once in his senior year in high school Kitty and I confronted Mark and asked him if he was drinking. "Do you want the truth, Dad?" he responded, "Or do you want to hear what you want to hear?"

I believe drinking contributed to Mark's fall in some way, at least impairing his balance and judgment. In my own mind I also feel Mark fell from the wall for two other reasons.

The first is that the wall itself was very dangerous and never should have been used as a short cut. The people who owned the apartment house and wall shouldn't have allowed it to become a Sigma Chi pathway as it had been for years. The day after Mark's fall, the apartment owners rushed to put up a wrought iron fence. They then hunkered down to wait for a lawsuit that never came. We learned later that the fraternity had asked them to put up a fence and the apartment owner told the fraternity to stuff it – to just not walk there.

Many lawyers approached us, particularly when the papers reported the UCLA connection and the lawyers saw the deep pockets of state government. We chose not to sue anybody. It would not bring Mark back, it would hurt the fraternity

Mark loved, and we had enough money already to fund the scholarship we wanted to set up in his name. Also, the prospect of depositions and reliving the experience held no appeal.

The second contributor to Mark's fall was what his mother called "those stupid boots," which he wore that night and loved so much as his mark of independence, and I guess a west LA mark of "cool."

Those cowboy boots now sit in our garage in a white plastic bag with black magic marker saying "Edler" written by a nurse in the UCLA emergency room. The bag was returned to us with his other clothes that night – pants ripped open in urgency, his shirt stained with blood around the collar, his brown boxer shorts, and those stupid boots with slippery soles and no tread.

We don't know whether to hate the boots because they helped kill him, or cherish them because he loved them so much. So unresolved, the boots sit in their plastic bag frozen between becoming convicted felons or a shrine to our child.

At the end of month six, July 27, Kitty turned 49. I didn't feel like giving her a present and she didn't feel like getting one.

Instead, I gave her a poem and, looking back, it marks a first sign that we were healing and determined to go on. In it I acknowledged the obvious – that we never would be the same people again, but that we would go on together. I reached back again to Rick's "we have to live our lives one-third better now" observation – a perspective that was taking over our lives. And I gave Kitty simply the gift of my next 30 years.

There was one more positive sign at six months. Kitty reluctantly began to wear her seat belt again.

Chapter Nine – Year One

In year one we began to build a new life that was to become very different from the old one we were leaving behind.

We were introduced to a unique organization called The Compassionate Friends, a worldwide support group for bereaved parents.

Several days after Mark died a long and wonderful friend who had lost a child a few years earlier called us from Connecticut and told us about the group. She also told us to go get a lock of Mark's hair before we buried him. We couldn't do the hair, it was just too much to ask. But we did hesitantly go to the national conference of Compassionate Friends a few months later in Charlotte, North Carolina.

Here we saw several thousand bereaved parents come together with only one thing in common – they had lost a child. Race didn't matter. Income didn't matter. Religion or politics or appearance didn't matter. This was truly the club with the highest membership dues in the world, and the one nobody wanted to join.

But once you qualified, you were welcomed without pretense, prejudice or masks. People were simply there to help each other survive.

We became very active in The Compassionate Friends. It was immediately helpful for Kitty, and more gradually helpful for me. On the first anniversary of Mark's death, we and a few special friends founded a new chapter in Southern California and called it South Bay/LA. We discovered that this was one thing we could do in Mark's name, and we were well qualified to do it. We were leaders, we were well organized, and we had "been there."

The Compassionate Friends was founded in 1969 by Rev. Simon Stephens, an English chaplain who discovered he could not fully comfort a couple in his care who had lost a child, but he did know of another couple who had lost a child earlier. So Reverend Stephens put the two couples together, and the formula worked. Today there are more than 650 chapters of TCF, as it is called, in 12 countries. It has no religious affiliation, and is simply a self-help organization offering friendship and understanding.

On the "outside," we found most people's reaction to hearing about our interest in a bereaved parent support group to be the same: "Why would you want to get together with a bunch of other parents who have lost children? Aren't you depressed enough already?" I can't blame people for feeling that way. I would have too.

The answer is threefold. First, the rest of the world does not want you to talk about your child after the first few months. They want you to be "over it." Compassionate Friends is a safe place where you can talk all you want to, and then listen to someone else's story too.

Second, Compassionate Friends is a group of people who can really help each other. They can honestly look another parent in the eye and say "I know how you feel" and establish an immediate credibility that someone on the outside, no matter how extensive their "professional training," simply cannot do. You have to have been there.

Third, TCF is a place where you can go to help somebody else in your own child's name. And helping someone else helps you heal. This is a basic truth about recovery from almost anything.

When you go into this valley, you change in other ways too. Your priorities in life and your sensitivity to what is going on around you is different. You no longer watch news the same way. The parade of violence – film at eleven – is no longer just numbing statistics. Each story makes you pause and think about the children and newly bereaved parents marking this day forever.

Mark died from a sudden fall. That death has much in common with other accidental deaths on the "news" like automobile accidents. One of the most common parental hurts in sudden deaths is the "I wish I hads." The things left unsaid like "I love you," or said in anger and now impossible to take back.

There are also the "If onlys." If only I had taken Mark to dinner that Friday night instead of driving out to the desert, maybe I would have changed his footsteps forever and he would be alive today. If only I had called. If only . . . .

When a child dies from an extended illness, the grief is different. The parents have the time to say good-bye to their dying child, but they also grieve twice – an extended and exhausting grief during the illness which often alters a family's pattern of living for months or even years before the death;

and then a second grief when the child actually dies, no matter how prepared they are in advance.

There is one other group among bereaved parents that is unique – parents who have lost their only child or all of their children at once and, in the eyes of the rest of the world, are now childless. This is especially difficult for parents in our support group who look at other bereaved parents and, even though they know better, still think: "Yes, you say you know how I feel, but how can you – you still have other children?"

Parents with other children at home have to return to the living no matter how deep their grief. There are still school lunches to pack, birthday parties to arrange, school parent-teacher conferences to attend, little league games to coach.

But the parents who have lost their only child go home to a silent house. Time stops, like the clock at Nagasaki. The child's room is often left untouched and memories sit undisturbed. Telephone calls stop. No children come by anymore. No voices are heard. No laughter. And the parents eat in silence, looking only at an empty chair at the table and at each other.

What do these parents do on Mother's Day or Father's Day? Are they still a mother and a father? Of course. But who sends them a card or flowers? In our Compassionate Friends chapter, we do. It is often the only card they get.

Halfway through year two Kitty claims she was at her absolute low point. Not the first month. Not six months. But eighteen months. I asked her why.

"Eighteen months after the death," she said, " is the time when everybody else has gone on with their own lives. Nobody talks about Mark or mentions his name any more. Even his friends have grown noticeably older in appearance, while we know Mark is staying the same age forever."

During this period Kitty's friends got her through it. I didn't. She developed a special bond with two other mothers who had lost children about the same time.

I needed a bond with another bereaved father. Luckily I found one too.

There is a special guilt reserved for fathers. There is a built in expectation that we fathers can "fix" anything. That's what we do. If the bike gets broken, we fix it. If the family gets lost on vacation, we find our way back to the highway without asking directions. If there is a noise in the house in the middle of the night, we get up and check it out. If our child dies, we make it all well. Except we can't. We can't fix it and we can't even comfort our wife, because we are torn apart too.

Trust me. This is bigger than all the machismo we fathers bring to the event. The death of our child knocks us for a complete loop. We can't gut ourselves through it. We can't make it all well. We can't work longer and harder at the office and work our way out of it. And we can't swallow hard and pretend it never happened. It is bigger than we are.

Two thirds of marriages in which a child dies end in divorce. I didn't believe such a statistic when I first heard it. I do now.

Chapter Ten — Year Two

In year two we faced our first Christmas at home. In year one the holidays simply didn't exist. We got out of town.

The little questions were the toughest. Do we hang up Mark's stocking? We did. Do you replay the old Christmas movies. We couldn't. Do you have Christmas dinner with the same good friends that you did before, but with a missing place at the table. We did.

Our close friends stood by us. But even then, the holiday chit-chat seemed meaningless and nobody mentioned Mark's name. So we did by including him in grace. Then other people relaxed and it was okay. We had said "the name" out loud.

It is the little things that sneak up when you don't expect them. During the holidays I was "catching up" and cleaning up loose ends in my home office. On my computer I had a rolodex which allowed me to call up any contact name, address and phone number. Going through it I came upon

Mark's listing with his college dormitory room and phone number. Obviously useless, I hit the "clear" button.

"Do you really want to delete Mark Edler?" came the computer prompt. I sat in my office staring at the screen crying silently, unable to move my hand.

In year two several major events occurred. We bought a new house and I lost my job.

With regard to the house, everyone gave us the same advice in the first few weeks: "Don't make any big decisions for a year." And we followed it.

I think it is good advice. Some people sell their house right away. Some people give away their child's things and months or years later regret it because they have no tangible memories to hold, no clothes to touch and smell.

I think two years is about right to go ahead with big decisions and it was right for us. We moved, but stayed nearby in the same community.

The house we sold was the house in which we had raised our boys. The move was a symbolic transition. It was a way of carefully packing one part of our life away, and beginning a new one.

Saying good-bye to Mark's room for the last time was something I thought a lot about. Like so many of the "big" things I worried about, it was easier than I had imagined.

I had already learned that it isn't the major events that get to you – like birthdays, anniversaries, and moving. It's the little things that happen unexpectedly and you aren't prepared for – like the computer prompt, or the T-shirt he loved that you find in the bottom of a drawer where he left it, or a note in his own handwriting with a long forgotten phone number, or his name and a smiley face drawn inside his textbook.

So as I took a last look at his room and said good-bye. I reasoned to myself that Mark is not here, it is just a room. Mark is the memory I am taking with me.

Still, I paused at the door to look back. I could see him lying in his bed, his phone cocked in one ear and the red quilt he loved on top of him.

"Goodnight Marcos," I said, as I had so many times before, making a fist pound in the air which was our little symbol. "Good night Popper," I recalled his answer.

At the end of year two I got fired. I didn't get laid off. I didn't leave to pursue other interests. I didn't go on special assignment. I didn't elect to take early retirement. I got fired.

I really don't know what I might have done differently at the office to have prevented it. I was working as hard as I possibly could, but not producing the results the company needed and deserved in its Los Angeles office. And, as the head of the office, there was no place to escape for even a short time.

I was adrift. My office windows overlooked the UCLA campus, and my commute exit each morning was a repeat of the last 5 minutes of my drive from the desert to the emergency room. I will always feel that I should have asked for a six-month leave of absence, and my boss would have given it to me. But such a step simply was not in my makeup at the time.

It was very hard on my self image to be fired. But there was also a strange quiet and peace that came with it. On my way back to Los Angeles from San Francisco, where I had gone to get the news, I realized I was going to miss the income but really not much else. For me, that particular fire had gone out.

On hindsight, it gave me the chance to start a new life. Without that push, I probably would have hung on to the financial security much longer. And it was the very process of re-inventing myself and my priorities that helped me walk out of the valley sooner.

I left my fast track career exactly at age 50. The birthday provided a convenient and ego-saving way to say good-bye to employees and a business I truly loved for 29 years.

At this low point in my life there was a high point too. I recall the saying: "When one door closes, another opens." At 50, for my birthday, Kitty prepared a wonderful surprise gift – a trip to Tahiti on our favorite cruise line, the Windstar. The Tahiti trip focused us on our future.

Sitting in Tahiti on Thanksgiving, 1993, I took stock of my life. I made a list of my blessings and my worries.

On the upside, I had Kitty and Rick, and 18 wonderful years with Mark. I had a wonderful family and had married into another. I had a renewed faith, 29 years in a fascinating career, good friends and several truly "best" friends, my health, a house overlooking the Pacific ocean, and enough money not to worry too much about tomorrow.

I also had something I loved to do and couldn't wait to get at each morning – a passion for writing and the time to do it. Reading my list back I was filled with overwhelming gratitude, not envy or grief.

I felt genuine excitement as I transitioned to a new third stage in my life. I would miss the power and prestige of running advertising agencies and going to black tie dinners. From a career standpoint, I was sorry not to have accomplished everything I wanted for my employer. But I was ready to leave it behind and start something new.

Yes, I had experienced a great tragedy. But none of us get to 50 without great joy and some pain. I would miss Mark and think about him every day for the rest of my life, but I was not going to camp in the valley.

By the end of year two I was beginning to climb my way out. Kitty was not there yet.

Chapter Eleven — Year Three

In the Spring of year three we decided to have a new fountain at our church dedicated to Mark. The minister, knowing of our desire, suggested a specific dollar contribution.

We thought about it and decided we could give the amount he asked relatively easily and without much pain. So we gave the church four times the amount, not to show off but because we knew this would mean a real commitment on our part to a place and a pastor that meant so much. To us this increased gift *was* a big deal, and we wanted it to be.

On May 22, 1994, I was invited to give the Sunday sermon at the dedication of the fountain. Several things stand out. My best friends came. I said what was in my heart. And the choir director, a wonderful and talented man who sang at Mark's service, had the choir wear their formal robes for the service. This touched me very deeply. It was a sign of honor and respect for the day.

The act of actually talking to the church congregation forced me to crystallize my thoughts about God and faith and what had really changed inside me.

Two and a half years ago I had been one of life's "skaters." I was sailing over life like a skater on a frozen pond. I looked around – a comfortable spectator, but not really a participant. For me, God was not dead, just irrelevant. He was the God of childhood "Sunday School," who wanted me to lead a "good life," but didn't really impact me much as head of an advertising agency.

Then my life changed forever and the skater fell through the ice.

Kitty and I don't skate over life any more. We feel it, like the cold water when the ice breaks. We feel for other people who hurt. We have developed an impatience with the trivial, which I suspect makes us less "nice" than we used to be.

In terms of God, I know Mark had intellectually worked it through. His writings tell me so. And in dying I feel he passed this on as a gift to his parents – and changed our faith forever from ritual to substance.

It may be easy to dismiss our "new found" faith as one born out of shock and necessity. Often people who experience a death are either brought closer to God or become angry with him, or both. Clearly, we wanted so badly to believe we would see Mark again, it could be argued, that we grasped any "straws" that suggested this was possible.

Frankly, there was some of that going on. But perhaps the death of our son was a also a "wake up call" that helped us see the obvious all around us.

There is no absolute proof of course. In his "Aquinas" essay Mark wrote "ultimately faith must be proven by faith itself." But I have found that quiet observation, an open mind, and simple common sense can take us farther than we might think. Briefly, here are some thoughts that helped me.

1. Simple historical precedent. Generations before us have believed in one God. And not just Christian. The basic beliefs of Judaism, Christianity, and Islam are in one God, the sanctity of human life, and a life hereafter. While these religions differ in the interpretation of their prophets – Moses or Jesus or Mohammed – they are united in the core belief that there is one God and good triumphs. Truly this belief, unlike any other, has "stood the test of time."

I am reminded of an analogy that I heard at a Compassionate Friends meeting: religion is the cup and spirituality is the coffee. Too many of us are walking around with empty cups when what counts is the coffee. I no longer care about the nature of someone else's cup, but care deeply that there is something in it.

2. A credible explanation for creation. This is sort of proof in reverse, but it has helped me. Is it any more incredible to believe in creation by a God, than to believe that we all evolved from a few paramecium swimming in the ocean? And, if you adopt evolution, then the Biblical version of God as the creator is still not threatened. Evolution may simply be "the way God does things."

And who caused the big bang in the first place? In his adult education classes Karl Johnson asks: "Who says to an embryo in a pregnant woman 'it's now time to grow the fingernails?"

Someone said that the miracles of nature do not seem to be miracles because they are so common. If no one had ever seen a flower, a dandelion would be the most startling event in the world. When asked about faith, Ralph Waldo Emerson

said: "Because of what I can see, I trust in what I cannot see."
It is one of my favorite quotes.

3. Near Death Experiences. Clearly, there is widespread
interest in this judging by best-selling books. Whatever the
details, the fact is that the "out-of-body" experience of almost
dying – the separation from body; floating in space, the
peaceful white light, and greeting at the end of the tunnel by
long deceased family or friends – is not an isolated
phenomena. It has been recorded by thousands of different
people who "almost died." It is the same story for adults and
little children in every language and on every continent
around the world.

I believe this is not coincidence. It is strong support for
believing in life after death. Dr. Elizabeth Kubler-Ross spent
a career caring for the dying. Her response to the question of
an afterlife is a resounding: "absolutely without doubt."

There is a rule if you are lost in a foreign country and need
directions always "ask three strangers – if two tell you to go
the same way then that is the way to go." Consider how
many total strangers have given us the "same directions"
about what happens when we die.

4. The law of the circle. I call it that because I think the circle is the "natural order" of things. Anyone need only look at the moon, the sun, the shape of the horizon at sea, a tree trunk, or the ripple of a drop of water in a lake.

Five hundred years ago men ignored the obvious in front of them and thought the earth flat. I think some people do that today about the existence of God and an afterlife.

Life is circular. It does not end. It is not linear. Just look at the obvious in front of our nose. The sun sets and rises again. Energy never gets "lost," but just changes form. Seeds become plants. Leaves do not die – they decay, become fertilizer for seeds, and are reborn again. Clouds become rain, become ocean, evaporate and rise, and become clouds again. Parents lead to children. Then children become parents. Nothing in nature just stops. Life everywhere goes on.

Dr. Kubler-Ross compares death to the simple shedding of a cocoon in which a person leaves the tired, injured or diseased body behind to emerge effortlessly into a new life. I like that analogy. It makes good old fashioned common sense. It is simple. It is truly the way the world seems to work. After death must be new life. A different form perhaps, but certainly new life.

5. "Intuition" that God is real. There is so much we don't understand. We really do seem to see "through a glass, darkly." Much of what we don't know, I think, lives in the realm of what we have come to call our right brain. The right brain is our creative half, but has no language. The logical and analytical left side has all the language. So the right side can't "talk" to you. It just "feels" things.

Have you ever met somebody and just felt you didn't like him, but couldn't say why. That's your right brain talking to you. We call it "intuition" or "a hunch," or "a gut feeling." Did you know Einstein never actually proved his theory of relativity. He just had a hunch it existed, and it was proved by others later on.

Why should we not trust these feelings as much as logic from our left side? Why not trust intuition, as much as analysis? I have a "hunch" that God exists. And I trust it.

These are a few thoughts that helped me. Of course Mark's death caused me to think more deeply about God, than I had in my entire life up until then. I came away absolutely convinced that, just as the earth is round but we couldn't see it in the 15th Century, there really is a God and the proof is all around us if we will only stop and notice.

Towards the end of year three – November 23, 1994 –Mark's 21st birthday came.

Do you celebrate a 21st birthday for a child who is no longer here? Of course not. Yet it was an important day in our world of "would have beens." Mark would have been 21 and he would be an official adult.

Kitty and I didn't know quite how to acknowledge the birthday. So, I wrote Mark a letter. I got the idea from one of my best friends, a man named Rich Gold. Every year on his son and daughters' birthday, Rich writes both children a letter, but they don't know about it. When each child turns 21, he will present them with a very special gift of 21 letters from Dad. Here is my letter.

Dear Mark,

You would have been 21 today. The whole family would be gathered around to celebrate this day you looked forward to so much. You would be president of your fraternity by now, finishing up your senior year at

UCLA, and planning the rest of your life. Instead, you are forever eighteen.

Mom misses you very much. Rick and I do too. But you and Mom had something very special. I pray that you will watch over her, love her, protect her, and help her live the rest of her life happy, despite such a large hole in her heart. Mom still works too hard. And she thinks of you every day – especially the late night talks you had together.

Jill is now at UCLA. I know you are proud of her. She went through rush and pledged Delta Gamma. She will never forget you. And at 20 she is beautiful, caring and everything you knew she would become.

Your best friends are seniors now. Greg is living uncomfortably alone in a role he expected you and he to play together. He has launched a beer company called California Prophet, with a label showing a young man standing silhouetted in the sunset holding a surfboard. The young man is you. Darin is now at UCLA too, and a Sigma Chi following your footsteps.

The year you died the Palos Verdes High School
volleyball team played the entire season with your
number eight on their sleeves. Your friend Matt Campisi
had your initials tattooed on his ankle. All of Team
Happy Face misses you.

I miss you too. I miss your love, your sense of humor,
your attitude towards life, and those hugs when you
were a little boy. I guess sometimes I miss those the
most. . . the motor home trip to Wyoming, Indian
Guides, your smile and your "Hi Popper" hello.

We suddenly have a very small family now. Just the
three of us.

Rick has grown so much. He is our rock. And he never
will forget you, even after Mom and I are gone.
Sometimes we all worry about Rick. He didn't ask to be
an only child. And he has the entire burden of the future
on his shoulders, living his life for all the Edlers.

I want to ask you to take care of your brother. He is
everything our family could be – quiet, kind, caring, and
a loving son and brother in an unfair world. If you are a

guardian angel, please make a special effort to be there for Rick.

I didn't do very well at the office after you died. I tried. I really think I did. But my world changed forever. And I couldn't hold it together. I feel very alone sometimes. My parents are gone and you are too. Mom is changed forever without you. I don't honestly know how I am doing.

I don't want Mom and I to become professional mourners. We can't live in the past. Yet we don't want to ever forget you, or any moment of our life together.

Happy Birthday, Son.

Love, Dad.

Chapter Twelve — Rick's Story

The waiting area at the UCLA Medical Center emergency room has four wall plugs, two sunset pictures with gold frames, four boxes of tissue, and eight chairs.

I didn't know this until three and a half years after Mark died. It came out in a conversation with Rick in which he shared his own feelings about the loss of his brother, and gave me permission to include his words here.

"Dad," he said, "I'm not a 'let it out' kind of guy. When I got to the emergency room that morning everybody was there, including some of your friends I didn't even know. And I had to act sad because everybody expected me to and kept looking at me and asking me how I was doing. So I just sat and stared at the room, looking like I thought I was supposed to look. I memorized the room while waiting for Mom and you to arrive. I can still see it clearly today."

Rick's story reminded me of something years ago. I was playing volleyball during a labor day block party in our neighborhood in Cincinnati. I fell and broke my foot and everybody rushed me to the hospital. Rick, then about three, was forgotten. Somebody put him on a back stair step, told him to wait there, and gave him a family size bag of potato chips.

While I was having my foot set in a cast, Rick was left alone with all those chips. He sat on the step for hours eating the whole bag. When we got home, he was really sick. Rick has never liked potato chips since. This time he was waiting for me again, but he was in the UCLA emergency room.

"Dad," he continued, "I remember Mom calling and I remember driving to UCLA. I stopped at a red light when I exited at Westwood and realized there was only one other car on the entire road and it was behind me. So I ran the light. The cop was at my door in seconds. He probably thought I was drunk. I told him gibberish about my brother and he said okay and walked away."

"Then I realized I had no idea where the emergency room was and the campus was huge. So I asked him and he told me to follow him. Every kids dream, including mine, is for a police escort. When it came, I didn't care."

"I had a very bad feeling during my drive. Mark had just finished hell week at his fraternity. Since I had been in a fraternity at USC, I knew what went on. I figured some stupid stunt at the house had caused an accident."

"When I arrived at the emergency room I remember being surprised that the cop just pulled away, and didn't hang around to check out my story. I guess he had called ahead."

"I first saw Mrs. Shapiro, Greg's Mom. Greg was sitting in a chair and would not look at me. 'What happened?' I asked. Greg would give it to me straight, I thought. People ran to get doctors and stuff like that. I repeated my question. But nobody would answer me."

"I knew then that Mark was dead. The first thing I heard was all this legal mumbo jumbo and disclaimers from the doctors about head trauma and how they had done everything they could . . . . Eventually someone said the words 'Mark passed away.' My first thought was how do I tell my parents?"

"I was also supposed to call you and Mom in your cars. Mom kept paging me. It was a catch 22. If I called you, you would know. If I didn't, you would suspect. I chose not to deal with it."

"Then Mom walked in. She looked at me. Someone ran to get the nurse and doctor again. I wasn't going to wait this time. It wasn't fair."

"Mark did not make it,' I said. 'Mark died.' I eliminated any risk of miscommunication."

"About ten minutes later you walked in, Dad. It was the first time I ever saw you totally lose it. I thought to myself, 'this is real.'"

Later, on his way home from the hospital, Rick stopped first at Mark's fraternity house. "I walked directly into Mark's room," Rick said, "His roommate was just getting up. 'Hey,' he said, 'who are you?'"

"I was Mark's brother,' I answered."

"What do you mean was?"

"He's dead."

"As I left he mumbled something about that not being funny. I know I should go back and apologize to him, but I never have."

"I drove the rest of the way home in anger. I yelled and screamed and red lined my Porsche. Later in the morning I cooled down and drove over to our house."

"I remember during the first few weeks how disappointed I was when I would pull up to the house and see lots of cars in the driveway. I knew I would have to put on my politically correct sad face. Then people I didn't even know were going to ask me how I was doing, or how I was dealing with it, or tell me how sorry they were and how important it was to let it out."

"I wanted to say, 'Please shut up and leave me alone.' Grief should have visiting hours so we also have time to be alone as a family. We didn't need any more potato salad."

"I had a lot of strength in those next few days. It came from my friends who just showed up, and it came from inside too. I felt Mark was there. He was helping me make all the decisions. He gave me insight and I felt it. A few months later I realized that feeling was gone. He had left. But he had been there to help me."

"It was really hard for me to see Mark in the hospital hallway, but it wasn't hard at the wake. That body wasn't really him as far as I was concerned. I no longer had a connection to it. All my friends were there and I wanted to smile and tell jokes and be with them, and not stand around and look sad. Mark would have wanted it that way."

"I remember walking outside the funeral home and seeing Mr. Campbell (a very close family friend) standing in the parking lot. He told me he couldn't go inside; that he wanted to remember Mark the way he was. I really respect Mr. Campbell for that."

"All the anticipated difficult times are not hard for me. I am okay on Mark's birthday and on holidays and so forth. I don't even mind hearing the songs I picked out for Mark's service."

"It's the stuff I don't expect that gets to me. That includes certain music when I really listen to the words for the first time. And, I still react when I see a black Pathfinder on the road. I speed up to see if Mark is driving. I know he isn't, but it doesn't matter."

"I'm okay and I'm still me. Some kids who go through this try to emulate their dead brother or sister. They pick up the slack, and act like him. I didn't do that."

"After Mark's death I actually felt superior to other people. I know that is a strange word to use, and I don't want to sound like I have a big ego. But I suddenly had a better and deeper understanding of life. I appreciated it more."

"I see people all the time who show disrespect for life. They have abused it. They sit on their butt and blame the world for all their problems. I have contempt for these people. I really get upset and angry. I want to say "Hey, this is not a big deal. Life and death is a big deal. Everything else is little stuff."

"I also feel bad for what I have lost. I will never be an uncle. I will not have Mark in my wedding. I will not see him graduate. Part of my life was taken away from me. A part of me died too."

"When people ask me if I have any brothers or sisters I say 'I had a brother.' Sometimes this sails on by and sometimes it stops the conversation. I enjoy talking about Mark but other people feel it is hard on me. It isn't. Not talking about him is what hurts."

About nine months after his death I went an entire day without thinking about Mark. I didn't realize it until the next day. Then I cried. I was afraid I was forgetting him and losing the memory of his voice and smile. I was angry with myself for letting a whole day slip by. Now I have moved past all that. I will never forget. It's just that every single day you cry and then one day you don't. One day you just don't think of him at all. One day it doesn't hurt as much. It takes time."

"My friends changed also. Two were especially important to me – Kevin and Tim. Kevin was about my age and had lost a brother. Kevin and I really didn't have a lot in common, but we could talk to each other. There is nothing like talking to someone who has been there. I think it was good for both of us."

"My friend, Tim also knew the value of life. He faced death, and survived. In high school he was burned over 30 percent of his body in an airplane crash. He has to wear long sleeve shirts for the rest of his life, which really sucks in Southern California."

"Right after Mark died Tim called me up from college and said he was going to take me to the Comedy Club. He drove down from college in Santa Cruz – a full six hours – to have dinner and see the show, and then drove back. He didn't ask me if I wanted to go. He just took me. I needed that."

"Tim and I developed a vocabulary – a shorthand between people. Others who try to help you mean well. But you can't say 'I know how you feel' if you haven't been there. Instead just say, 'I'm here for you."

"For me it took two years to recover. The first six months were a blur. In a year I was coming back. Two years were full circle."

"But I changed. When I'm driving on a freeway, I don't look at funeral processions as a nuisance anymore. I feel for the people in the front car. I feel more in touch with life in my mid-twenties now than people I see at 50 or 60. I read about people who are dying or are old and complain that life is slipping away. AIDS patients say this, but it is too late for them. In a way Mark gave me a wonderful gift – I appreciate life right now. I don't have to wait until I'm 60 or have some disease."

"And I feel the three of us became a stronger family going through this together. It was a very fragile time. I think the camel's back was very weak, and any straw would have broken it. But there was no straw. If you and Mom had been fighting or drinking or splitting up, I think it would have put me under."

"My biggest fear used to be letting you and Mom down by not being successful enough. Now my biggest fear is loneliness. One day you both will die and I will be left alone. I never imagined that could happen. I surround myself with my friends and every night I have to talk to someone. I have to know I am not alone."

"I am not afraid to die. I don't fear it. I know it's coming some day. I don't want to rush it, but I respect it."

"I don't even feel funny being on the UCLA campus. I guess I feel like I have a special birthright to be there even though I went to USC. When I date UCLA girls I am surprised when, after a few dates, they make the connection. 'Oh, that was your brother!' It sort of gives me celebrity status."

"Mark would like that a lot."

Chapter 13 — Year Four

On August 8, 1995 – well into year four and our 30th wedding anniversary – Kitty and I were in Rome, a stopover on our way to a Greek island cruise. It was our first real vacation with no business strings attached in a long time.

While touring in Rome we recognized the piazzas we visited with the boys 11 years ago when we toured Europe on a Eurail Pass and, as a family of four, crammed 12 countries into 14 days. In Rome back then we didn't even stay overnight. We just came into the train station – slam, bang did a whirlwind tour of the coliseum and Gucci's (the longer line) and got back on the train.

This trip was different. We were here without the boys. On a tour of the Sistine Chapel, Kitty spotted a little plastic coliseum on the table of a street vendor. "Look," she said, "that's the souvenir Mark bought."

And sure enough, eleven years earlier, Mark had bought a plastic coliseum, taken it home to California, and filled it with nickels and pennies ever since. It was one of the special things in his room when we cleaned it. I had forgotten. Kitty never does.

The street vendor shouted "Hey, lady. You like coliseum? Special price." Quietly Kitty said, "Gratzi, we already have one," and walked tearfully on. Losing a child comes back sometimes when you least expect it. And traveling around the world doesn't make it go away. You carry it with you.

Flashbacks like that become a part of your new self. For Kitty it was thoughts of different happy events – every time she drives by the little league field, by the intermediate school, or when she sees a child who looks like Mark at an earlier age.

Part of coping with loss is taking those special memories and bringing them back into your conscious in a positive way, and having them available for you whenever you want them. I like to think of it as not just putting memories in a drawer, but opening that drawer regularly and taking them out, holding them in your hands, and enjoying them. Too many people shut the drawer forever.

I know everyone's time table is different. But I think the grief process for the loss of a child takes at least three years. You go into the valley, pass through stages of shock, anger, guilt, disorganization, and reorganization, and come back out again on the other side. You never forget and you never "get over it," but you do come out.

Nobody goes through these stages in perfect order and there is no "right time" to be at any particular stage. Many people go back and forth, one day in reorganization and then dropping back the next to anger or disorganization. But the real point is that eventually the griever does return to life.

But in the case of the loss of a child, parents never come out of the valley at the same place or as the same people that went in. We are changed forever.

It's almost as if grief mounts a radar antenna on your head, even though you never wanted it there. That antenna scans the world around you with a new clarity and a sensitivity to others you never had before. It gives you x-ray vision into other people's hurt.

Most people rearrange their priorities in life. Many strengthen their faith. Some change careers, do more charity work, or find a cause with special meaning. These are all positive steps we take in our children's name. It doesn't make the hurt go away, but it helps us heal.

There was a time I felt I would never heal, have a new life, or even have my wife back. I did not resent it. I accepted it. I accepted that the person I loved and who also smiled and laughed and enjoyed each day with me was probably gone forever. When I was coming out of it, she simply wasn't.

It took a almost four years for Kitty to climb out of the valley, but she did. She started in year two caring a little if she lived or died. By the end of year three, she began to take care for her health, her looks and the house again.

It was about this time when Kitty started to look different, and better. I made a comment one day and she looked at me in surprise: "Didn't you notice I just started wearing my contacts again?"

Kitty had not worn her contacts for three and a half years – since Mark died. And I hadn't noticed one way or the other. It was like coming home from the office and not noticing the furniture had been rearranged, only worse.

The truth is I wasn't looking at anything physical in my marriage partner. I just didn't care any more than she did. We were living on autopilot, and passing in the hallway. If sex happened occasionally it was between two machines fulfilling a basic need, and then going to sleep. Nobody was home upstairs.

After the death of a child most women say they not only have no interest in sex, but it actually becomes distasteful. Sex is associated either with making children or pleasure, and a grieving mother wants neither.

Grief eventually can bring couples closer together, and it did for us. But it took a lot of time, and a lot of patience with each other. Some days Kitty would be up and I would be down. Sometimes she needed to talk and I wanted a silent dinner. If I missed going to the cemetery, Kitty could anger me by suggesting that I was somehow "overdue" for a visit. I would then remind her of the Compassionate Friends rule: we all grieve differently and there is no right or wrong way.

A few times we would be in the middle of an argument over something totally insignificant and one of us would look at the other and simply say: "I miss him too."

One of the positive signs on the other side of the valley is the ability to genuinely experience pleasure again – sexual and otherwise – and not to fake it. It is the ability to go out to dinner, to enjoy friends, to tell a joke, and to laugh out loud for real. It is to ultimately realize that life is still good and you don't have to be miserable to honor your child's memory. You don't have to feel guilty about feeling happy.

In year four I was able to stop and assess my walk through the valley with some measure of hindsight. Here is what I see from where I stand near the rim on the other side.

Kitty and I now divide our lives into two parts: before Mark died and after Mark died. We don't like ourselves as well in the first part, yet would trade all that we have to go back.

In the second part we have tried to be better people; to give back in gratitude for the joy of the life we have had, the joy of Rick, and the joy of 18 years with Mark. We are not bitter, but count what we had, not what we lost.

We both feel we are living more on purpose, with a sense of what really matters. We are doing things that count beyond money, and trying to help others in Mark's name. Of all the "universal truths" of grief, the one most true is simply this: the more you give back to others, the more you heal.

We have also decided it's okay to be selfish, too. We have learned to say "no," to a party we don't really want to go to. We have learned to take time for ourselves without feeling guilty. We have learned to enjoy the moment and the people that surround us, not to worry so far ahead into a future that may suddenly not be there. We now stop and pick the daisies.

We have accepted the fact that Mark is dead and that our most important wish can't come true. In doing that, we are no longer afraid of death. We don't want to die, but we do not fear it.

We have a sense of inner peace which I know my father had, and which I was unable to understand when he died in Asheville. If I had it to do over, I would have handled my last visits with Dad in a very different way. I would have talked about Mom and God and told him I loved him right up close and personal. But I don't have it to do over.

Kitty and I both changed our personality, too.

I became more of a loner. In truth, I have always been a loner, but running an advertising agency made that impossible. It is a business of gregariousness where ideas come from the flint of striking people against each other. You can't run an advertising agency behind a desk with your office door closed, and I never did.

Kitty became a truly nicer person. She reaches out constantly through Compassionate Friends, goes to meetings of our chapter when I am suffering from grief overload, and patiently takes the phone calls that never stop coming from newly bereaved parents.

Kitty and I both joined the church where Mark's service was held, and with her Jewish upbringing, Kitty became a better Jew and Christian than I ever will be. She simply ignores religious protocol and organizational doctrine, and gets on with a grief ministry to which she feels called.

In addition to Compassionate Friends, we began facilitating a "grief support" group twice a year at our church, helping people in the community deal with the death of any loved one. Usually the attendees are new widows or widowers. But occasionally a newly bereaved mother or father will walk in with "the stare," and we know immediately.

We also value each other more. On our 30th anniversary Kitty told me that she loved me when we were married, but she loves me more now. That meant a lot. I feel the same way about her.

We suffer fools poorly. We don't care much for superficialities. We are tired of beige people. We know the value of time and refuse to waste it.

We value our good friends more. They were there for us when we needed them, and we will never forget. And we have made new friends at a substance level that seems to count. My rolodex has gone from more than a thousand names to less than a hundred.

When we meet people we are no longer looking over their shoulder to see who else is in the room. We simply don't care, and by concentrating on the person in front of us, I think we have expanded our ability to be more interesting people too.

In short, we have returned to life. Of course we will never forget Mark. But we are going to go on and try to live a better life in his name – one-third better.

Sometimes Kitty just stops and shakes her fist in the air and says "I have to lead a better life. Otherwise, what will I say to Mark when I see him?"

We have absolute confidence we will see Mark again. We just don't know quite how it will all work.

And most of all we celebrate every single day with our son, Rick. He is more than there for us. He actually likes being with us, or is a remarkable actor. And we count our hours in terms of how many are left until we can see him for a Sunday night dinner.

I know deep down that there was a relationship between Kitty and Mark that I never had. In fact, I have come to believe that there is a special relationship between all mothers and their sons; just as I feel there must be that same special relationship between daughters and fathers.

Recently, I found Kitty watching a movie by herself and, although the movie was a comedy, she was in bed crying. "Mark and I used to watch movies like this," she said, "after you had gone to bed. And," she added, "I have so long to wait until I can be with him again."

If I had one wish for this book, it would be to reach every mother and father to remind them that all children are on loan. I would ask these parents to always make time for their kids, even when the career and homemaking and social pressures are the greatest. And I would wish for them to get to know what I call the three selves of their child.

The first self, I think, is where you deal with your kids every day. It is the self that comes home late, talks too long on the phone, and "mouths off." It is the self that never picks up his clothes, wants "things," doesn't seem to appreciate what it has, or care enough about others. This "self" is always in a hurry, always "going out, " and always hungry.

The second self is very important, and most parents get at least a glimpse of it. It is the side your child's best friends know. It is the self you love deeply, and only comes out when you sit down together and absolutely commit yourself to listen instead of "tell." It is the side of your child that comes out on the third day of a forced "family vacation." It's the self that surprises you with deep wisdom, and your "where did that come from?" reaction. I think grandparents often see this side before parents.

The third self of your child is the one that someone, someday, will fall in love with and marry. This self is where love and hope and faith are growing. This side of your child rarely comes out in front of a "parent," expecially during the teen age years.

It is the side of the "athlete of the year" that also writes poetry you haven't seen yet. It is the side that chooses a state university because it wants to be around people who are not all from the same economic "class." It is the side that loves sunsets, and would have told you so if you only had asked.

It is the side that, if you lost that child suddenly, you would grieve most for not having known better.

Work hard to know that "third self" of your child. I can guarantee you absolutely that it is there.

Recently, on that vacation in Greece in the middle of year four, Kitty got out a swim suit she had not worn in a long time. She remarked: "You know, Rich, I remember when I bought this. It was before Mark died."

There it was again – the one defining demarcation in our lives, with all the world's time falling forever into pre or post.

It will always be that way.

I don't know how I know. I just know.

Epilogue

In 1996 I published my first book, *If I Knew Then What I Know Now*. It is a collection of hindsights from business leaders each answering the same one question: "What do you know now that you wish you knew 25 years ago?"

The book was a labor of love, and dedicated to Mark.

In March I was signing books at a shopping mall near Los Angeles and noticed a lady quietly standing in the back. After about two hours most people had left, and she hesitantly approached my table. Without saying anything, she slid a small white card across the table. I looked at her, somewhat puzzled, and read the card:

> Mr. Edler.
> My daughter Sharyl Seward is the LA City firefighter who ministered to your son. She would be honored to talk with you if you ever wish to.

Her daughter's phone number followed.

I stood up and hugged the mother. She explained that she had seen a newspaper feature about the book, and recognized my name and story from things her daughter had told her four years ago. She came to the signing to introduce herself, but was hesitant because she did not know how I would react. She said she didn't want to upset me, so she waited until everyone was gone.

Through her daughter Kitty and I learned about the "missing" twenty minutes we could never fill in – the last minutes of Mark's life. This is what Sharyl told us:

> I was one of six on the LA Fire Department rescue team when we got the call. I was the first one to Mark. He was lying there alone, just like he was sleeping straight on his back, arms at his sides.
>
> Mark was unconscious and not breathing. I performed CPR. As I was doing chest compressions I was increasingly touched by him – he was dressed so neatly – his clothes, jeans, shirt, cowboy boots, plus manicured nails, and in the prime of life.

We put a collar around his neck and put him on a backboard and stretcher. While transporting him in the ambulance we brought him back but lost him in the emergency room shortly after he was transferred. In the emergency room they opened up his chest and massaged his heart.

He was a UCLA student. I have only brought UCLA students into the university medical center a few times and the medical staff always seems to go the extra mile to help one of "their own." Mark was greeted at the door by lots of doctors when we arrived – they were ready for him.

Everyone wanted him to make it and prayed for him. He was special. That night deeply affected me. I have a stepson his age. He looked like every parent's dream for their child. We all tried so very hard to keep him alive.

And I know he didn't suffer. I was with him.

These were the words we had waited four years to hear. Our final steps out of the valley.